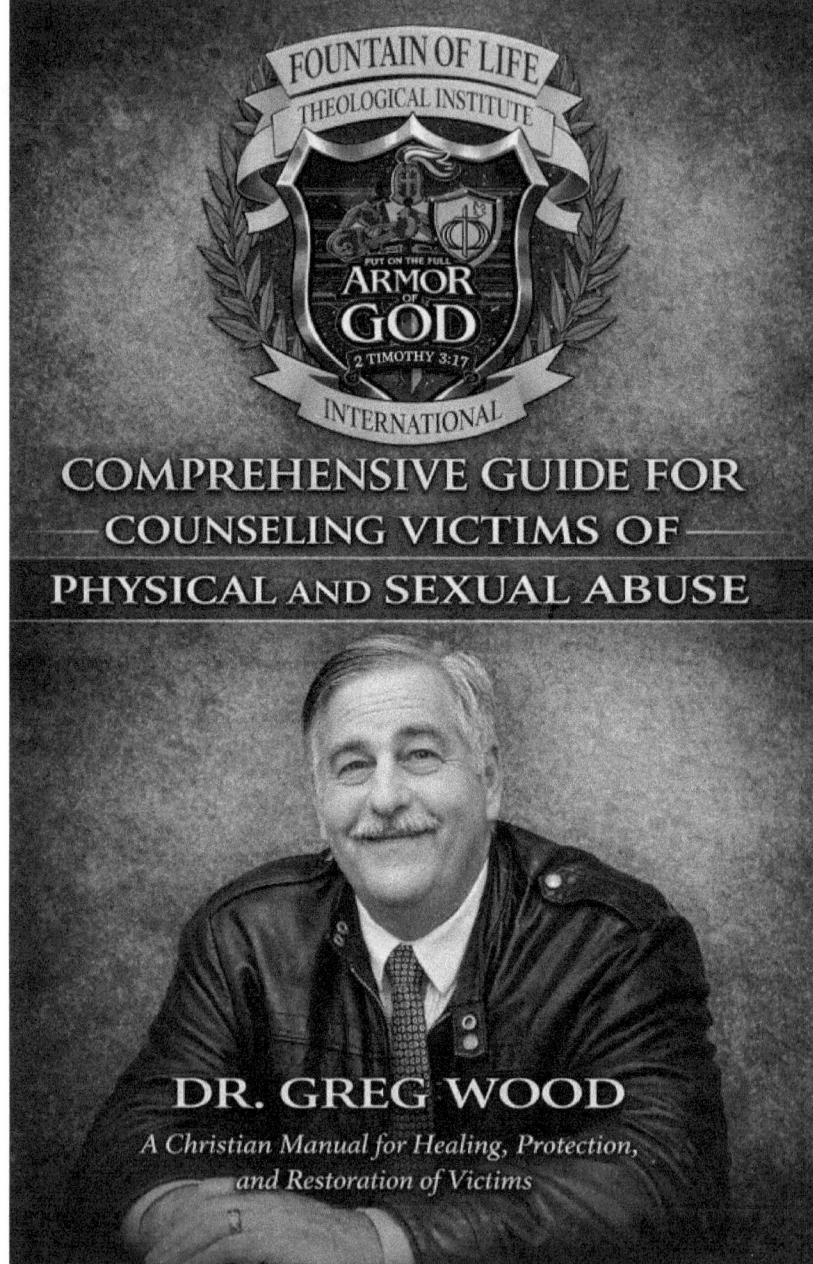

Comprehensive Guide for Counseling Victims of Physical and Sexual Abuse
A Christian Manual for Healing, Protection, and Restoration
By
Dr. Greg Wood

Fountain of Life Theological Institute International

© 2026 Dr. Greg Wood. All rights reserved.

No part of this book may be reproduced, stored in a retrieval system, or transmitted in any form or by any means electronic, mechanical, photocopying, recording, or otherwise without the prior written permission of the publisher, except in the case of brief quotations in critical articles or reviews.

Scripture quotations are taken from the *King James version of the Bible*, used with permission. All rights reserved.

This book is intended as a **pastoral and counseling resource**. It does not replace professional medical, psychological, or legal services. Readers are encouraged to seek appropriate professional assistance when necessary.

Dedication

To all survivors of abuse:

May this guide remind you that your voice matters, your life has immeasurable worth, and your healing is precious to the heart of God.

And to the counselors who walk alongside them; thank you for being Christ's hands and feet in the darkest valleys.

Acknowledgments

I wish to thank the many survivors whose courage to share their stories has inspired this work. Your voices are not silenced; they echo as testimonies of resilience and hope.

Special gratitude to pastors, counselors, and advocates who faithfully defend the vulnerable. Your service reflects the character of Christ, who said: *"Let the little children come to me, and do not hinder them, for the kingdom of heaven belongs to such as these"* (Matthew 19:14).

Above all, I give thanks to the Lord Jesus Christ, the Great Shepherd, who restores souls and makes all things new.

Preface

Abuse is one of the gravest wounds a person can endure. It scars the body, shatters the soul, and shakes the very foundations of trust. Yet, as devastating as abuse is, the gospel proclaims that healing and restoration are possible in Christ.

This guide was written to equip Christian counselors, pastors, and caregivers with biblical wisdom, practical tools, and ethical foundations to minister effectively to survivors of physical and sexual abuse. It is not a substitute for professional therapy or legal justice, but a companion resource that integrates **spiritual care with practical guidance**.

As you journey through these pages, may you be reminded that counseling is not just about methods, it is about the heart of Christ being expressed through you.

In a time when the cries of the abused are often silenced, this book is a prophetic voice reminding the church of its sacred duty: to defend the vulnerable, protect the weak, and guide the broken toward healing in Christ.

Dr. Greg Wood has created not only a theological framework but also a practical manual for counselors. Rooted in Scripture and filled with wisdom, this work will serve as a lifeline for both survivors and those who walk alongside them.

This is more than a book; it is a call to action.

Chapter 1: Introduction

The Role of the Christian Counselor in Abuse Recovery

1.1 The Weight of the Call

Working with survivors of physical and sexual abuse is one of the most sacred and demanding responsibilities a counselor can undertake. This guide is not written merely for professionals, but for pastors, lay leaders, Christian therapists, and believers who sense the Spirit's call to "bind up the brokenhearted" (Isaiah 61:1).

Survivors do not simply carry emotional pain; they often carry **generational trauma**, **spiritual confusion**, and **psychological scars** that ripple into every area of their lives. Counselors must be prepared for long journeys of healing rather than quick solutions.

The Apostle Paul reminds us: *"Bear one another's burdens, and so fulfill the law of Christ."* (**Galatians 6:2**)

This burden-bearing is at the heart of Christian abuse counseling.

1.2 Biblical Foundations of Healing

God's Heart for the Oppressed

- *"He executes justice for the oppressed and gives food to the hungry. The LORD sets prisoners free."* (**Psalm 146:7**)
- *"Do not rob the poor, because he is poor, or crush the afflicted at the gate; for the LORD will plead their cause."* (**Proverbs 22:22–23**)

The counselor represents God's compassion and justice. Survivors need to see that God does not overlook their suffering, nor does He condone the evil done against them.

Christ as the Healer of Trauma

Jesus Himself endured violence, betrayal, abuse, false accusations, physical torture, and crucifixion. He identifies with survivors not as a distant figure but as One who *knows their pain*. Hebrews 4:15 assures us: *"We do not have a high priest who is unable to sympathize with our weaknesses."*

The Work of the Holy Spirit

- The Spirit **comforts** (John 14:26)
- The Spirit **intercedes** when words fail (Romans 8:26)
- The Spirit **restores identity** (Romans 8:16)

Thus, Christian counseling is not merely talk therapy but Spirit-led partnership.

1.3 Understanding Trauma Through Scripture and Psychology

What is Trauma?

Psychologically, trauma is an overwhelming event or series of events that leaves a person feeling powerless, unsafe, and broken. Abuse is uniquely traumatic because it involves **betrayal of trust**, often by someone close (parent, spouse, clergy, authority figure).

Common trauma responses:

- **Hypervigilance** (constantly scanning for danger)
- **Avoidance** (numbing or denying memories)
- **Flashbacks** (reliving abuse through sensory triggers)
- **Dissociation** (feeling detached from one's body or emotions)

Trauma in Biblical Narratives

- **Tamar (2 Samuel 13):** She lived with shame and devastation after sexual assault.

- **Joseph (Genesis 37–50):** Betrayed and abused by his brothers, yet God redeemed his pain.
- **Job:** Though not abused, he suffered deep emotional trauma, crying out for justice and restoration.

These stories remind survivors that **their pain is not hidden** from God.

1.4 The Unique Calling of the Christian Counselor

More Than a Therapist

While secular therapy offers important techniques (CBT, EMDR, trauma-informed care), the Christian counselor adds:

- **Biblical worldview** – understanding sin, evil, justice, grace.
- **Spiritual care** – prayer, scripture, deliverance from lies.
- **Eternal hope** – healing that looks beyond this life.

Roles of the Counselor

1. **Healer:** Helps integrate fragmented emotions.
2. **Shepherd:** Provides spiritual covering and guidance.
3. **Advocate:** Connects clients with safe housing, medical care, and legal support.
4. **Intercessor:** Prays fervently for breakthrough.

1.5 Challenges Counselors Will Face

- **Disclosure Shock:** Hearing disturbing details without showing judgment.
- **Counter-transference:** Managing your own emotional reactions.

- **Spiritual Warfare:** Recognizing that abuse often has demonic oppression attached.
- **Resistance:** Survivors may minimize, deny, or rationalize abuse.
- **Burnout Risk:** Counselors may absorb secondary trauma if not careful.

Paul's exhortation in **2 Corinthians 1:4** guides us: *"[God] comforts us in all our affliction, so that we may be able to comfort those who are in any affliction."*

1.6 Case Study

Case: Maria (pseudonym)

Maria, a 24-year-old, revealed that her stepfather abused her for years. She feared that God was angry with her. Her symptoms included nightmares, panic attacks, and self-harm.

Counselor's Approach:

- **Initial sessions:** Focused on safety and trust. No pressure to share details.
- **Validation:** "Maria, you are not to blame. God hates what happened to you."
- **Spiritual re-framing:** Reading **Psalm 34:18** ("The Lord is near to the brokenhearted").
- **Practical step:** Connected her with a women's shelter for temporary safety.
- **Progress:** Over months, Maria learned grounding techniques for anxiety and began journaling prayers. Eventually, she testified that she sensed God's presence for the first time in years.

This illustrates how **clinical care + biblical care = holistic healing**.

1.7 Reflection Questions for Counselors

1. How do I personally react when I hear stories of abuse? Do I feel overwhelmed, angry, or numb?
2. Do I truly believe God can restore even the most broken survivor? Why or why not?
3. Have I developed a support system for my own emotional health as I counsel survivors?
4. Am I willing to confront injustice, even if it means involving authorities?

1.8 Practical Tools for Chapter 1

- **Grounding Prayer for Sessions**:
  "Lord, make me an instrument of Your healing. Let my presence reflect Your love, my words reflect Your truth, and my silence reflect Your listening heart."
- **Counselor's Checklist Before Beginning Abuse Work:**
    - Do I know the **mandatory reporting laws** in my state?
    - Do I have referral contacts for **medical, legal, and emergency services**?
    - Do I have a mentor or supervisor for **accountability and debriefing**?
    - Am I prepared spiritually (prayer, fasting, boundaries)?

Chapter 2: Understanding Abuse

Defining the Reality and Breaking the Myths

2.1 What is Abuse?

Defining Abuse

Abuse is the misuse of power and control over another person that results in harm. It is not simply an isolated act of anger, it is a pattern of domination, manipulation, and exploitation.

- **Physical Abuse:** The intentional use of physical force that results in bodily injury, pain, or impairment. This includes hitting, kicking, slapping, choking, burning, restraining, or using weapons.
- **Sexual Abuse:** Any sexual activity forced, coerced, or manipulated against a person's will. This includes rape, molestation, sexual harassment, exploitation, incest, pornography involvement, and grooming.

Key Point: Abuse is never about love. It is about power, control, and exploitation.

2.2 Common Myths and Misconceptions

Survivors often remain silent because of cultural, family, or religious myths. As counselors, we must confront these lies with truth.

Myth #1: "Abuse only happens in broken or non-Christian homes."

- **Truth:** Abuse occurs across all social, cultural, and religious groups. Many survivors are found within church communities.

Myth #2: "If the victim didn't fight back, it wasn't really abuse."

- **Truth:** Many victims freeze in fear (trauma response). Submission does not equal consent.

Myth #3: "If there are no bruises, it wasn't abuse."

- **Truth:** Sexual abuse and psychological abuse often leave invisible wounds deeper than physical scars.

Myth #4: "God hates divorce, so victims must stay."

- **Truth:** God hates violence against His children (Malachi 2:16). Scripture never condones remaining in harm's way. Safety is godly.

Myth #5: "The abuser just has an anger problem."

- **Truth:** Abuse is not a "loss of control." It is a calculated attempt to maintain dominance.

Scripture Response: *"Woe to those who call evil good and good evil"* (**Isaiah 5:20**). Counselors must not minimize or spiritualize abuse.

2.3 The Cycle of Abuse

Psychologists describe a repeating pattern in abusive relationships:

1. **Tension-Building Phase:** Stress increases. Victim feels like they are "walking on eggshells."
2. **Incident Phase:** Abuse occurs — physical assault, sexual violation, verbal attack.
3. **Reconciliation Phase (Honeymoon):** Abuser apologizes, gives gifts, promises change.
4. **Calm Phase:** Period of peace where victim believes things

have improved — until tension builds again.

Biblical Parallel: Pharaoh's cycle of oppression in Exodus mirrors this — promises of relief, followed by more cruelty. Abuse is often repetitive unless confronted.

2.4 Psychological and Spiritual Impact of Abuse

Emotional Impact

- Fear, anxiety, panic attacks
- Shame and guilt
- Depression and suicidal thoughts
- Low self-worth and identity loss

Spiritual Impact

- Survivors may ask: "Where was God?"
- They may feel dirty, unworthy, or unforgivable.
- They may mistrust spiritual leaders if abuse occurred in religious contexts.

Scriptural Truths:

- *"The Lord is close to the brokenhearted"* (**Psalm 34:18**)
- *"You are precious in my eyes, honored, and I love you"* (**Isaiah 43:4**)

2.5 Recognizing the Signs of Abuse

Counselors must learn to discern both obvious and hidden indicators.

Physical Signs:

- Bruises, burns, unexplained injuries
- Frequent "accidents" with vague explanations
- Wearing long sleeves in hot weather to cover marks

Behavioral Signs:

- Withdrawn, fearful, or hypervigilant
- Sudden changes in grades or work performance
- Reluctance to go home
- Low self-esteem or self-blame

Spiritual Signs:

- Guilt or shame in prayer
- Feeling unworthy of God's love
- Avoiding fellowship or church due to fear or secrecy

2.6 Case Example

Case: James (pseudonym)

James, a 35-year-old man, sought counseling for anger issues. As sessions progressed, he revealed that he had been sexually abused by a teacher as a child. He never told anyone because "boys are supposed to be strong."

Counselor's Observations:

- James masked pain with aggression.
- He struggled with intimacy in marriage.
- He doubted God's goodness.

Counselor's Approach:

- Validated his trauma and named it as abuse.
- Introduced scripture on God's protection of the vulnerable

(Psalm 91).
- Used trauma-informed techniques to help him process suppressed memories.
- Encouraged him to share his story in a safe men's group for accountability and healing.

Result: James began to see himself not as weak, but as a survivor with God-given dignity.

2.7 Reflection Questions for Counselors

1. Do I sometimes minimize abuse by calling it "just a marital conflict" or "discipline gone too far"?
2. Am I willing to challenge cultural or church myths that keep victims trapped?
3. Have I examined my own biases about gender, power, or sexuality that might influence my counseling?
4. Can I recognize the difference between anger management issues and intentional abuse?

2.8 Practical Tools for Chapter 2

Quick Screening Questions (to ask carefully and privately):

- "Do you feel safe at home?"
- "Has anyone ever touched you in a way that made you uncomfortable?"
- "Has someone ever forced you to do something sexual against your will?"
- "Do you feel afraid of your partner (or family member)?"

Counselor's Checklist:

- Avoid blaming questions ("Why didn't you leave?").
- Always affirm: *"You are not to blame for what happened."*
- Know referral resources: hotlines, shelters, legal aid.
- Document carefully and confidentially.

2.9 Closing Exhortation

As counselors, we must remember that **naming abuse is the first step toward breaking its power.** Survivors often need someone to validate their story with truth. Jesus said in **John 8:32**: *"You will know the truth, and the truth will set you free."*

In this chapter, we have seen that abuse thrives in secrecy and silence. Counselors are called to bring truth, compassion, and biblical clarity.

Chapter 3: The Psychological and Spiritual Impact of Abuse

Healing the Mind, Heart, and Spirit

3.1 Introduction

Abuse leaves more than bruises. While the physical wounds may fade, the psychological and spiritual scars often remain long after. Survivors struggle not only with the trauma of what was done to them but also with distorted beliefs about themselves, others, and God.

As counselors, we must understand both the **psychological effects** (trauma, PTSD, depression, anxiety) and the **spiritual effects** (shame, doubt, anger toward God, distorted faith). Our role is to minister to the whole person; body, soul, and spirit.

3.2 The Psychological Effects of Abuse

Trauma Responses

- **Hypervigilance:** Constantly scanning for danger; jumpy and unable to relax.
- **Flashbacks & Nightmares:** Reliving abuse through intrusive memories.
- **Dissociation:** Feeling disconnected from body or surroundings, as if the abuse is happening to "someone else."
- **Avoidance:** Fear of people, places, or conversations that trigger memories.

Scripture Parallel: David described symptoms of trauma in **Psalm 55:4-5**:
"My heart is in anguish within me; the terrors of death have fallen upon me. Fear and trembling come upon me, and horror overwhelms me."

Emotional Consequences

- Depression, hopelessness, and suicidal thoughts.
- Difficulty regulating anger or emotions.
- Self-harm as a coping mechanism.
- Addiction (alcohol, drugs, pornography) as a way to numb pain.

Relational Consequences

- Fear of intimacy, even in marriage.
- Difficulty trusting authority figures.
- Isolation from family, friends, or church.
- Repetition of abusive patterns in relationships.

3.3 The Spiritual Effects of Abuse

Distorted View of God

Survivors often wrestle with questions like:

- "Where was God when I was being abused?"
- "Does God love me, or am I cursed?"
- "Why did God let this happen?"

If the abuser was a spiritual leader, the survivor may associate God with betrayal.

Guilt and Shame

Shame is one of the deepest wounds. Survivors often feel "dirty," "unworthy," or "damaged." Yet Scripture teaches the opposite:

- *"If anyone is in Christ, he is a new creation"* (**2 Corinthians 5:17**)
- *"There is therefore now no condemnation for those who are in Christ Jesus"* (**Romans 8:1**)

Broken Faith
Some survivors withdraw from prayer, worship, or fellowship. Others continue outward religious practices but inwardly feel abandoned.

As counselors, we must gently restore the survivor's relationship with God by separating **God's character** from the evil acts committed by people.

3.4 Case Examples
Case 1: Sarah (Pseudonym)
Sarah, a 42-year-old survivor of childhood sexual abuse, struggled with recurring nightmares and avoided intimacy with her husband. She believed God was punishing her. Through counseling, she learned that her abuse was not her fault. Reading **Psalm 139** restored her sense of worth - she realized she was "fearfully and wonderfully made." Over time, her marriage began to heal.

Case 2: Daniel (Pseudonym)
Daniel, a man in his 50s, had endured years of physical abuse from his father. He developed alcoholism to numb his pain. In counseling, he processed his grief and anger, learning to forgive without excusing the abuse. Memorizing **Romans 12:2** helped him "renew his mind," replacing destructive coping mechanisms with prayer and accountability.

3.5 Counseling Strategies for Psychological Healing

1. **Create Safety First**
   Survivors cannot process trauma while feeling unsafe.
   Counselors must establish trust, confidentiality, and stability.
2. **Validate Experiences**
   Simple affirmations like, *"I believe you,"* and *"It was not your*

fault" are powerful antidotes to shame.
3. **Teach Grounding Techniques**
   - Breathing exercises for panic attacks.
   - Journaling to externalize pain.
   - Quoting scripture during flashbacks (e.g., Psalm 23:4).
4. **Encourage Healthy Coping Skills**
   Replace destructive coping (self-harm, substance abuse) with healthy alternatives: prayer walks, support groups, creative expression, and scripture meditation.

3.6 Counseling Strategies for Spiritual Healing

1. **Rebuilding the Image of God**
   Survivors need to rediscover God as loving Father, not as a reflection of their abuser. Passages such as **Isaiah 41:10** ("Fear not, for I am with you...") reassure them of His presence.
2. **Separating God from the Abuse**
   Clarify that God grieves over abuse. Evil people choose sin, but God promises to redeem brokenness (Romans 8:28).
3. **Guided Prayer and Scripture Reading**
   Introduce survivors to Psalms of lament (Psalm 13, 22, 88). These validate raw emotions while keeping faith anchored in God's character.
4. **Restoring Worship**
   Survivors may resist church. Allow them to take small steps — listening to worship music, writing prayers, attending safe gatherings.

3.7 Reflection Questions for Counselors

1. How do I respond when a survivor says, "God abandoned me"?
2. Do I rush people toward forgiveness without allowing space for grief and anger?
3. Am I trained to recognize PTSD symptoms and know when to refer to a specialist?
4. How can I integrate scripture naturally into trauma counseling without using it as a "band-aid"?

3.8 Practical Tools for Chapter 3
Worksheet: Identifying Lies vs. Truth
Survivors often internalize lies. Use this tool in sessions.

Lie Believed	Biblical Truth	Scripture
"It was my fault."	"You are blameless in Christ."	Ephesians 1:4
"I am dirty."	"You are washed, sanctified, justified."	1 Corinthians 6:11
"God abandoned me."	"I will never leave you nor forsake you."	Hebrews 13:5
"I am worthless."	"You are precious and honored in My sight."	Isaiah 43:4

Prayer for Survivors
"Lord Jesus, You see every wound and every hidden scar. Speak truth where lies have taken root. Restore dignity, break shame, and remind Your child that they are loved, chosen, and never forgotten. In Your name, Amen."

3.9 Closing Exhortation
The psychological and spiritual impact of abuse can feel overwhelming, both for survivors and counselors. Yet healing is

possible. As Isaiah 61:3 declares, God gives *"a crown of beauty for ashes, the oil of joy instead of mourning, and a garment of praise instead of a spirit of despair."*

Counselors must walk with patience, empathy, and prayer - trusting that the God who raised Christ from the dead can bring life out of even the deepest trauma.

Chapter 4: The Counselor's Role
Creating Safety, Building Trust, and Knowing Your Limits

4.1 Introduction

A counselor who works with survivors of physical and sexual abuse is walking on sacred ground. The survivor is entrusting you with their deepest wounds, often for the first time. Your role is not to "fix" them quickly, but to **create an environment where healing can unfold** through God's presence, wise counsel, and safe relationships.

Jesus modeled this in His ministry:

- He listened with compassion (John 4 – the Samaritan woman).
- He spoke truth with gentleness (Luke 7 – the sinful woman anointed His feet).
- He created space for the broken to be restored without shame (Mark 5 – the woman with the issue of blood).

As counselors, we reflect Christ's ministry of safety, presence, and restoration.

4.2 Creating a Safe Space
Physical Safety

- Confidential, private counseling setting.
- Clear boundaries about session length, location, and confidentiality.
- Written agreements about privacy (with exceptions for danger or mandatory reporting).

Emotional Safety

- Survivors must feel believed, not doubted.
- Avoid shock, judgment, or pressuring for details.
- Affirm: *"You are safe here. You are believed. You are not alone."*

Spiritual Safety

- Use scripture carefully; not as a weapon ("you must forgive now"), but as comfort.
- Provide opportunities for prayer, but never force spiritual practices.

Key Scripture: *"A bruised reed He will not break, and a smoldering wick He will not quench."* (**Isaiah 42:3**)

4.3 Establishing Trust

Trust is the foundation of all trauma recovery. Survivors of abuse have often had their trust shattered by people closest to them.

Ways to Build Trust:

- Be consistent (show up on time, follow through on promises).
- Be transparent (explain your role, what will happen in sessions, when you must report).
- Listen more than you speak.
- Respect survivor's pace - let them decide what and when to share.

Trust-Killing Mistakes to Avoid:

- Minimizing their pain.
- Sharing their story with others.

- Over-spiritualizing ("Just pray more, and it will go away").
- Breaking promises.

4.4 Recognizing Your Limits

Counselors must walk in humility. You cannot meet every need, and trying to do so may cause more harm.

Know When to Refer

- **Medical Care:** If physical injuries or chronic health issues are present.
- **Psychiatric Support:** If PTSD, suicidal ideation, or severe dissociation emerge.
- **Legal Protection:** When safety or children are at risk (mandatory reporting applies).
- **Shelter and Social Services:** If the survivor has nowhere safe to go.

Proverbs 11:14 reminds us: *"Where there is no guidance, a people falls, but in an abundance of counselors there is safety."*

4.5 Avoiding Re-Traumatization

Sometimes counselors unintentionally cause harm by mishandling disclosures. Survivors may feel re-violated if pressured, judged, or dismissed.

Do Not:

- Push for graphic details too early.
- Use accusatory questions ("Why didn't you run?").
- Quote scripture in a way that blames (e.g., "You must forgive or God won't forgive you").
- Treat the survivor as a "case" instead of a person.

Do Instead:

- Allow survivors to control the pace.
- Validate emotions: *"It makes sense you feel afraid/angry/confused."*
- Normalize trauma reactions: *"What you are experiencing is a normal response to a terrible situation."*
- Introduce scripture as gentle reminders of God's care.

4.6 Ethical and Legal Responsibilities
Confidentiality

- Explain clearly what confidentiality means and when it cannot be maintained.
- Example: *"What you share is private, unless you are in danger, someone else is in danger, or the law requires me to report."*

Mandatory Reporting

- Every state/country has laws requiring reporting of child abuse, elder abuse, or threats of harm.
- Counselors must know local laws to protect survivors and themselves.

Documentation

- Keep secure, factual notes (avoid personal opinions).
- Document disclosures factually: who, what, when, where.
- Protect survivor identity in storage and sharing.

4.7 Case Example

Case: Lydia (pseudonym)

Lydia, age 28, disclosed sexual abuse by her step-uncle. She feared that if she told anyone, her family would reject her.

Counselor's Role:

- Created a safe, confidential space.
- Explained the limits of confidentiality.
- Allowed Lydia to set the pace of disclosure.
- Provided referral to a trauma therapist specializing in sexual abuse recovery.
- Prayed with Lydia, affirming God's love and safety.

Result: Lydia began to rebuild trust, first in the counselor, then slowly in God and safe people around her.

4.8 Reflection Questions for Counselors

1. Do I clearly explain confidentiality and reporting before sessions begin?
2. How do I personally respond when I feel overwhelmed by a survivor's story?
3. Do I have referral contacts ready (shelters, lawyers, doctors, trauma therapists)?
4. Am I able to sit with survivors in silence, without rushing them?

4.9 Practical Tools for Chapter 4

Counselor's Session Checklist

- Begin with prayer (if survivor is comfortable).
- Review confidentiality boundaries.
- Ask open-ended, non-leading questions.
- Validate and affirm survivor's worth.

- End with grounding (breathing, scripture, prayer).

Grounding Scriptures for Safety

- *"The Lord is my rock, my fortress, and my deliverer."* (Psalm 18:2)
- *"I will both lie down in peace, and sleep; for You alone, O LORD, make me dwell in safety."* (Psalm 4:8)
- *"God is our refuge and strength, a very present help in trouble."* (Psalm 46:1)

4.10 Closing Exhortation

The role of the counselor is not to rescue but to **walk alongside survivors with Christ's compassion and truth**. By creating safety, building trust, and knowing your limits, you prepare the soil where the Holy Spirit can bring deep healing.

Paul's words in **2 Corinthians 1:3–4** summarize this calling:

"Blessed be the God and Father of our Lord Jesus Christ, the Father of mercies and God of all comfort, who comforts us in all our affliction, so that we may be able to comfort those who are in any affliction, with the comfort with which we ourselves are comforted by God."

Chapter 5: Assessment and Identification

Recognizing, Screening, and Responding to Signs of Abuse

5.1 Introduction

One of the greatest challenges in counseling is that **most abuse remains hidden**. Survivors often live in silence due to fear, shame, manipulation, or threats. For this reason, counselors must become skilled in **assessment and identification**.

Jesus modeled discernment in His ministry. He could perceive what was hidden in people's hearts (John 2:25). While we are not omniscient, counselors are called to develop both **clinical wisdom** and **spiritual sensitivity** to recognize abuse that may not be openly disclosed.

5.2 Warning Signs of Abuse

Physical Indicators

- Unexplained bruises, burns, cuts, or injuries.
- Frequent medical visits with vague explanations.
- Wearing long clothing in hot weather to hide marks.
- Sudden weight loss or gain due to stress or neglect.

Behavioral Indicators

- Fearful, anxious, or withdrawn behavior.
- Flinching at sudden movements.
- Reluctance to go home or be around certain people.
- Dramatic mood swings or emotional numbness.
- Running away from home repeatedly (especially in teens).

Sexual Abuse Indicators

- Difficulty walking or sitting.
- Knowledge of sexual behaviors inappropriate for age.
- Sudden avoidance of a specific person.
- Sexualized behavior or language.
- Nightmares, bed-wetting, or sleep disturbances.

Spiritual Indicators

- Belief that God has abandoned them.
- Intense shame and guilt tied to religious beliefs.
- Fear of church leaders or authority figures.
- Statements like: "God hates me" or "I am unforgivable."

5.3 Asking the Right Questions

Survivors rarely disclose abuse directly unless they feel safe. Gentle, open-ended questions allow them to share at their own pace.

Principles of Asking

- Always ask in private.
- Use calm, non-judgmental tone.
- Avoid leading questions (don't put words in their mouth).
- Reassure: *"You don't have to answer anything you're not comfortable sharing."*

Sample Screening Questions

- "Do you feel safe at home?"
- "Has anyone ever hurt you physically?"
- "Has someone touched you in a way that made you uncomfortable or afraid?"
- "Is there anything happening in your relationships that you are afraid to talk about?"

- "Do you ever feel controlled or trapped by someone close to you?"

Responses to Disclosure

- Say: *"I believe you. This was not your fault. Thank you for trusting me."*
- Do not say: *"Are you sure?"* or *"Why didn't you stop them?"*

5.4 Documentation

Accurate, confidential documentation protects both the survivor and the counselor.

Guidelines for Documentation

- Record **facts only** (avoid assumptions).
- Use survivor's own words in quotes when possible.
- Note **date, time, and place** of disclosure.
- Document visible injuries factually (not "she looked abused," but "bruises noted on left arm, circular in shape").
- Store records securely (locked cabinet or encrypted file).

Avoid

- Sharing details with unauthorized persons.
- Mixing personal opinions into notes.
- Over-documenting unnecessary personal details.

5.5 Mandatory Reporting
What It Is

Mandatory reporting laws require counselors, clergy, teachers, and medical professionals to report suspected abuse of minors, elders, or vulnerable adults.

Biblical Support for Reporting

- Proverbs 31:8–9: *"Speak up for those who cannot speak for themselves... defend the rights of the poor and needy."*
- Ephesians 5:11: *"Have nothing to do with the fruitless deeds of darkness, but rather expose them."*

Steps to Reporting

1. **Know Your Law:** Each state/country differs. Counselors must be familiar with local requirements.
2. **Inform the Survivor:** If safe, tell them: *"Because I care about your safety, I need to make a report."*
3. **Report Factually:** Provide only necessary information to authorities.
4. **Support After Reporting:** Offer presence, prayer, and reassurance.

Important Note

Reporting does not end the counselor's role. Survivors need ongoing care and spiritual support even as legal processes unfold.

5.6 Case Example

Case: Maria (pseudonym)

Maria, age 15, disclosed to her youth pastor that her stepfather "comes into her room at night." The pastor recognized this as a disclosure of sexual abuse.

Steps Taken:

- Pastor reassured her: *"This is not your fault. Thank you for*

telling me."
- Documented her words verbatim.
- Contacted child protective services (mandatory reporting).
- Connected Maria with a safe shelter and counseling.
- Continued to meet weekly with Maria for prayer and emotional support.

Outcome: Maria began her healing journey, no longer in danger, and with ongoing Christian support.

5.7 Reflection Questions for Counselors

1. Am I able to recognize subtle warning signs of abuse, or do I wait for explicit disclosure?
2. Do I know the reporting laws in my area?
3. How would I handle my own emotions if a survivor disclosed something shocking to me?
4. Do I have a plan for what to do immediately if a disclosure happens in session?

5.8 Practical Tools for Chapter 5
Sample Intake Checklist

- Confidentiality explained
- Ask safety question: "Do you feel safe at home?"
- Observe physical signs (bruises, injuries, clothing)
- Note emotional signs (fear, withdrawal, hypervigilance)
- Document verbatim disclosure
- Know referral contacts (police, shelters, hotlines)

Safety Planning Tool
Work with the survivor to create:

- Safe people they can call in an emergency.
- Places they can go if threatened (shelters, friends, relatives).
- Code words for children or friends to signal danger.
- Emergency bag with essentials (ID, money, clothes).

5.9 Closing Exhortation

Assessment and identification are about **listening, watching, and protecting**. Survivors cannot always name their abuse, but as counselors, we are called to notice, ask, and act.

Jesus said in **Matthew 18:6**: *"If anyone causes one of these little ones who believe in me to stumble, it would be better for them to have a large millstone hung around their neck and to be drowned in the depths of the sea."*

God takes abuse seriously. As His servants, we must be vigilant, courageous, and compassionate in identifying and addressing it.

Chapter 6: Counseling Strategies

Practical Approaches for Healing Mind, Body, and Spirit

6.1 Introduction

Survivors of abuse need more than advice; they need **safe presence**, **skilled listening**, and **spiritual restoration**. Counselors must integrate **psychological best practices** with **biblical truth** to bring wholeness.

Paul wrote in **1 Thessalonians 5:23**:

"May your whole spirit and soul and body be kept blameless at the coming of our Lord Jesus Christ."

This verse reveals the holistic nature of healing. Abuse damages all three areas - spirit, soul, and body - and counseling must address each.

6.2 Core Principles of Abuse Counseling

1. **Safety First**
    - Healing cannot occur in an unsafe environment.
    - Counselors must help survivors establish physical, emotional, and spiritual safety.
2. **Pace of the Survivor**
    - Survivors must set the speed of disclosure.
    - Forcing details can retraumatize.
3. **Validation**
    - Survivors need to hear:
        - "I believe you."
        - "This was not your fault."
        - "You are not alone."
4. **Trauma-Informed Approach**
    - Understand how trauma affects the brain (fight, flight, freeze).
    - Use grounding exercises when panic or flashbacks occur.

5. **Biblical Integration**
    - Use scripture as comfort, not as pressure.
    - Help survivors separate God's character from human sin.

6.3 Listening Without Judgment
Why Listening Matters
Survivors often silence themselves for years. Listening with patience restores dignity.

James 1:19 instructs:
"Let every person be quick to hear, slow to speak, slow to anger."

Practical Listening Skills

- Maintain eye contact, but don't stare.
- Use calm body language.
- Repeat back what they share to confirm understanding:
  "What I hear you saying is that you felt unsafe..."
- Avoid clichés like "It will all work out."

6.4 Validation and Affirmation
Abuse often convinces survivors they are worthless. Counselors must counteract these lies.

Affirmations to Use in Sessions:

- "You are precious to God."
- "Your story matters."
- "What was done to you was evil, but you are not evil."

Scripture Support:

- *"You are precious in my eyes, and honored, and I love you."* **(Isaiah 43:4)**

- *"The Lord is near to the brokenhearted and saves the crushed in spirit."* (**Psalm 34:18**)

6.5 Trauma-Informed Techniques
Grounding Exercises

- **5-4-3-2-1 Technique:** Name 5 things you see, 4 things you feel, 3 things you hear, 2 things you smell, 1 thing you taste.
- Breathing: Inhale slowly, exhale with scripture (e.g., breathe in *"The Lord is my Shepherd,"* breathe out *"I shall not want"*).

Journaling
Encourage survivors to write letters to God, record prayers, or process memories safely.

Scripture Meditation
Guide them to meditate on verses like **Romans 8:38–39** ("nothing can separate us from the love of God").

6.6 Dealing with Shame and Guilt
Shame is one of the most crippling effects of abuse. Survivors believe they are "dirty" or "broken."

Counseling Approach

- Replace shame with truth through scripture.
- Example exercise: Have survivors write the lies they believe ("I am worthless") on paper. Then, write the biblical truth ("I am God's workmanship" – Ephesians 2:10) on another paper. Destroy the lie paper in a symbolic act of release.

6.7 Addressing Anger and Forgiveness
Survivors often wrestle with anger - at the abuser, at themselves, even at God.

Healthy Anger Expression

- Teach that anger is not sin by itself (Ephesians 4:26).
- Encourage safe outlets: journaling, prayer, physical activity.

Forgiveness

- Clarify that forgiveness is a **process**, not instant.
- Forgiveness does not mean excusing or reconciling with the abuser.
- Emphasize that forgiveness is about **freedom from bitterness**, not release from justice.

6.8 Integrating Scripture in Counseling

Do:

- Use scripture as comfort, not pressure.
- Share stories of biblical survivors (Joseph, Tamar, Job).
- Teach God's promises of healing.

Don't:

- Force verses like "forgive 70 times 7" prematurely.
- Use scripture to silence anger or grief.

6.9 Case Example

Case: Anita (pseudonym)

Anita, a 30-year-old survivor of childhood sexual abuse, struggled with panic attacks. She felt God hated her.

Counselor's Approach:

- Taught grounding exercises during panic attacks.
- Validated her pain: *"God did not cause your abuse. He grieves with you."*
- Guided her through Psalm 23, line by line, applying it to her story.
- Encouraged her to journal prayers when she couldn't speak them aloud.

Outcome: Anita gradually reduced panic episodes, found comfort in scripture, and began leading a small women's Bible group years later.

6.10 Reflection Questions for Counselors

1. Do I listen more than I speak in sessions?
2. Am I able to sit with silence, or do I rush to fill the space?
3. How do I balance validating pain with pointing to biblical hope?
4. Have I ever used scripture as a "band-aid"? How can I avoid this?

6.11 Practical Tools for Chapter 6
Sample Counseling Session Flow

1. Begin with grounding prayer (if survivor agrees).
2. Review safety and confidentiality.
3. Open floor for survivor to share.
4. Validate experiences (affirmation).
5. Introduce coping tools (breathing, scripture, journaling).
6. Close with prayer, grounding, or reflection exercise.

Affirmation Scripture Cards

Create small cards survivors can carry:

- "I am fearfully and wonderfully made" (Psalm 139:14).
- "I am chosen and dearly loved" (Colossians 3:12).
- "Nothing can separate me from God's love" (Romans 8:38–39).

6.12 Closing Exhortation

Counseling survivors of abuse requires patience, gentleness, and Spirit-led wisdom. Our strategies are not about quick fixes, but about restoring dignity, identity, and faith step by step.

Jesus said in **John 10:10**: *"The thief comes only to steal and kill and destroy. I came that they may have life and have it abundantly."*

Through compassionate listening, validation, trauma-informed care, and biblical truth, counselors can help survivors reclaim the abundant life Christ promises.

Chapter 7: Working with Survivors of Sexual Abuse

Restoring Dignity and Rebuilding Identity

7.1 Introduction

Sexual abuse is one of the deepest violations a human being can endure. Unlike other forms of abuse, it attacks not only the body but also the survivor's **sense of identity, intimacy, and dignity**. Because sexuality is tied to God's design for covenant and intimacy, sexual abuse distorts what God intended for good.

Counselors must approach survivors of sexual abuse with **extreme gentleness, patience, and biblical clarity**. Survivors often feel shame, guilt, or even responsibility for what happened. The counselor's role is to reaffirm:

- "You are not to blame."
- "What was done to you was evil, but you are not evil."
- "God still calls you beloved."

7.2 Understanding Grooming and Manipulation

Many survivors did not recognize their abuse at the time because abusers often **groom** their victims.

What is Grooming?

Grooming is the process of building trust, dependency, and secrecy to prepare a victim for abuse.

Common Grooming Behaviors:

- Gaining trust of family/community.
- Offering gifts, attention, or special privileges.

- Isolating the victim from others.
- Normalizing inappropriate touch.
- Threatening consequences if victim tells.

Why Survivors Feel Confused

- They may have felt "special" at first.
- They may fear people won't believe them.
- They may feel complicit, though they were manipulated.

Scriptural Truth: *"For nothing is hidden that will not be made manifest, nor is anything secret that will not be known and come to light."* (Luke 8:17)

7.3 Addressing Sexual Shame

Sexual abuse often leaves survivors feeling "dirty," "damaged," or "unworthy." Shame silences many for decades.

Counselor's Role

- **Name the abuse:** "What happened to you was wrong. You are not guilty."
- **Separate identity from abuse:** "You are a child of God, not what was done to you."
- **Affirm bodily dignity:** Remind survivors that their bodies are still temples of the Holy Spirit (1 Corinthians 6:19).

Biblical Reframing

- Tamar's story in 2 Samuel 13 reminds us that scripture acknowledges sexual abuse and its devastation.
- Yet, God restores dignity: *"Instead of your shame you shall have double honor"* (Isaiah 61:7).

7.4 Restoring Healthy Boundaries

Sexual abuse destroys boundaries. Survivors may struggle with:

- Saying "no."
- Trusting appropriate touch.
- Confusion between intimacy and exploitation.

Practical Strategies

- Teach survivors to identify safe vs unsafe touch.
- Role-play scenarios of saying "no" with confidence.
- Reinforce that consent is biblical (Song of Solomon 8:4 – *"Do not awaken love until it pleases"*).

7.5 Working with Children and Adolescents

- Use simple language ("bad touch," "good touch").
- Create space for play therapy or drawing as expression.
- Involve safe caregivers when appropriate.
- Always prioritize mandatory reporting and safety planning.

Matthew 19:14 reminds us: *"Let the little children come to me… for the kingdom of heaven belongs to such as these."*

7.6 Healing for Adult Survivors

Adult survivors may struggle with:

- Marital intimacy issues.
- Sexual avoidance or hypersexuality.
- Guilt or shame in Christian marriage.
- Mistrust of authority figures.

Counseling Goals:

- Help survivors separate abuse from God's design for sex.
- Address distorted beliefs (e.g., "Sex is always dirty").
- Work with couples if marriage is affected (with consent).

7.7 Case Examples

Case 1: Rachel (Pseudonym)

Rachel, age 26, was molested by a family friend. She felt dirty and avoided intimacy with her husband.

Counselor's Approach:

- Validated her pain and named it as abuse.
- Introduced Psalm 139 to affirm her worth.
- Worked gradually on trust-building exercises with her spouse.
- Encouraged couple's prayer for healing.

Outcome: Rachel slowly began to experience marital intimacy as safe and sacred again.

Case 2: Michael (Pseudonym)

Michael, age 40, revealed he was abused as a child by an older cousin. He believed it "made him weak."

Counselor's Approach:

- Helped him confront the grooming process and recognize he was not at fault.
- Addressed his belief system with scripture: *"When I am weak, then I am strong"* (2 Corinthians 12:10).
- Connected him to a men's support group.

Outcome: Michael overcame isolation and began speaking to other men about his story, breaking stigma.

7.8 Reflection Questions for Counselors

1. How do I respond when a survivor expresses sexual shame?
2. Do I truly understand grooming, or do I sometimes blame survivors for "not speaking up"?
3. Am I comfortable discussing sexuality from a biblical perspective without embarrassment?
4. How can I help survivors reclaim God's design for sexuality as holy and beautiful?

7.9 Practical Tools for Chapter 7
Affirmation Statements for Survivors

- "My worth is not defined by my abuse."
- "God calls me beloved, chosen, and clean."
- "I can set boundaries that honor God and protect me."

Healing Scriptures

- *"You are altogether beautiful, my love; there is no flaw in you."* (Song of Solomon 4:7)
- *"I will restore to you the years that the locust has eaten."* (Joel 2:25)
- *"Instead of your shame there shall be a double portion."* (Isaiah 61:7)

Symbolic Healing Exercise

Ask the survivor to bring a small stone representing shame. In session, read Psalm 103:12 (*"as far as the east is from the west..."*). Then encourage them to throw the stone into water as a physical act of release.

7.10 Closing Exhortation

Survivors of sexual abuse often feel they are beyond redemption. But the gospel declares that nothing is beyond God's healing. The counselor's role is to restore dignity, reaffirm identity, and point to God's redeeming love.

As Jesus said to the woman caught in adultery (John 8:11): *"Neither do I condemn you; go, and sin no more."* Though she was shamed publicly, Christ restored her dignity privately.

So it must be with survivors - counselors reflect the heart of Christ by affirming, protecting, and restoring.

Chapter 8: Working with Survivors of Physical Abuse

Restoring Safety, Strength, and Dignity

8.1 Introduction

Physical abuse is the **deliberate infliction of bodily harm** through hitting, slapping, kicking, choking, restraining, or otherwise injuring another person. While bruises and scars may heal, the **psychological terror and spiritual confusion** can last much longer. Survivors often live in fear, shame, and isolation, believing they must endure silently.

Counselors must affirm from the start:

- Physical abuse is never justified.
- Abuse is not "discipline," "stress," or "anger management." It is **sinful domination**.
- Survivors have the right - and biblical permission - to seek safety.

Psalm 72:14 declares: *"From oppression and violence he redeems their life, and precious is their blood in his sight."*

8.2 Recognizing the Dangers of Physical Abuse

Common Behaviors of Abusers

- Hitting, slapping, punching, choking.
- Restricting movement (locking in rooms, restraining).
- Using weapons or threats of weapons.
- Destroying property to intimidate.
- Controlling finances, phone access, or transportation.

Why Survivors Stay

- Fear of retaliation if they leave.
- Financial dependence.
- Concern for children.
- Misinterpreted religious beliefs ("God hates divorce").
- Hope that the abuser will change.

Cycle of Abuse (Revisited)

- Tension → Incident → Honeymoon → Calm → Repeat.
  This cycle must be explained so survivors see the pattern.

8.3 The Counselor's Role in Safety Planning

The counselor's first priority is always **safety**.

Steps in Safety Planning:

1. **Identify Safe People**: Friends, family, pastors who can be trusted.
2. **Safe Places**: Shelters, churches, community centers.
3. **Emergency Preparedness**:
   - Keep an escape bag (ID, keys, money, important papers).
   - Know emergency contacts and hotlines.
   - Establish code words with children or friends to signal danger.
4. **Legal Protection**: Restraining orders or police involvement if necessary.

Proverbs 22:3: *"The prudent sees danger and hides himself, but the simple go on and suffer for it."*

8.4 Helping Survivors Process Fear and Anger

Fear

Abuse instills deep fear. Survivors often fear their abuser will retaliate, or that God will condemn them for leaving.

Counseling Strategies:

- Remind them: *"God has not given us a spirit of fear, but of power, love, and a sound mind"* (2 Timothy 1:7).
- Teach grounding techniques for panic attacks.
- Affirm that leaving abuse is not sin but wisdom.

Anger

Survivors may wrestle with anger toward the abuser, themselves, or God.

Counseling Strategies:

- Normalize anger as a natural response to injustice.
- Teach healthy expression (journaling, exercise, prayer of lament).
- Guide them through biblical lament (e.g., Psalm 13).

8.5 Establishing Biblical Boundaries

Many survivors confuse "submission" with enduring violence. Counselors must clarify that biblical submission never condones abuse.

Key Scriptures for Boundaries

- *"Husbands, love your wives, as Christ loved the church and gave himself up for her."* (Ephesians 5:25)
- *"Do not be yoked together with unbelievers."* (2 Corinthians 6:14)

- *"Do not associate with a man given to anger."* (Proverbs 22:24)

Boundaries are godly because they protect life and dignity. Survivors can say **"no"** to harm while still saying **"yes"** to God.

8.6 Case Examples

Case 1: Laura (Pseudonym)

Laura's husband frequently hit her during arguments. She believed God wanted her to "endure."

Counselor's Approach:

- Showed her Malachi 2:16, which condemns husbands who "cover their garments with violence."
- Helped her create a safety plan and connect with a shelter.
- Reinforced: *"God values your life more than keeping an abusive marriage intact."*

Outcome: Laura left the abusive environment, pursued counseling, and began rebuilding her sense of worth in Christ.

Case 2: Samuel (Pseudonym)

Samuel, age 14, came to school with bruises. He finally disclosed that his father beat him regularly.

Counselor's Approach:

- Documented and reported abuse (mandatory reporting).
- Reassured Samuel that God did not approve of his suffering.
- Connected him with a foster family and trauma-focused therapy.

Outcome: Samuel found safety and slowly regained trust in authority figures.

8.7 Reflection Questions for Counselors

1. Do I sometimes spiritualize endurance, encouraging survivors to "pray harder" instead of prioritizing safety?
2. How comfortable am I with helping a survivor build a safety plan?
3. Do I know local resources (shelters, legal aid, hotlines) to connect survivors with immediately?
4. How do I handle my own fear when I hear about ongoing physical violence?

8.8 Practical Tools for Chapter 8
Safety Plan Worksheet

- Safe people I can call: _____
- Safe place I can go: _____
- Emergency code word: _____
- Items in my emergency bag: _____
- Important phone numbers: _____

Affirmation Scriptures for Survivors of Physical Abuse

- *"God is our refuge and strength, an ever-present help in trouble."* (Psalm 46:1)
- *"When I am afraid, I put my trust in You."* (Psalm 56:3)
- *"The Lord will fight for you; you need only to be still."* (Exodus 14:14)

8.9 Closing Exhortation

Survivors of physical abuse often feel trapped between fear of leaving and fear of staying. The counselor's role is to stand as a **voice of safety, truth, and hope.**

God's heart is never for His children to be harmed. He calls His people to rescue the oppressed and break the chains of violence. Counselors, therefore, must balance **compassion with action**, guiding survivors into both safety and healing.

Isaiah 1:17 sums up the call:

"Learn to do good; seek justice, correct oppression; bring justice to the fatherless, plead the widow's cause."

Chapter 9: Crisis Intervention

Responding to Immediate Danger with Wisdom and Compassion

9.1 Introduction

Crisis intervention is the **first line of defense** when a survivor is in immediate danger. While much counseling focuses on long-term healing, there are moments when a counselor must act swiftly to ensure safety.

Crisis situations include:

- Ongoing physical or sexual abuse in the home.
- Immediate threats of violence or harm.
- Suicidal thoughts or self-harm behaviors.
- Situations where children or vulnerable adults are at risk.

The counselor's response in these moments can be the difference between **safety and further harm**.

9.2 Principles of Crisis Intervention

1. **Safety First**
    - Immediate safety takes priority over long-term counseling.
    - Survivors must be removed from danger before healing can begin.
2. **Stay Calm**
    - Survivors may mirror your emotional state.
    - Respond with calm reassurance, not panic.
3. **Empower, Don't Control**
    - Survivors need to feel they have choices.
    - Provide options and resources, but let them make decisions when possible.

4. **Legal and Ethical Duty**
    - Counselors must comply with mandatory reporting laws.
    - Failure to act may put lives in danger and violate legal obligations.

9.3 Immediate Steps in a Crisis
Step 1: Assess the Danger

- Ask: *"Are you in danger right now?"*
- Determine whether the abuser is nearby.
- Evaluate risks for children or vulnerable individuals.

Step 2: Ensure Immediate Safety

- If in imminent danger, call emergency services (police, ambulance).
- If possible, help survivor relocate to a safe space (shelter, trusted friend).
- Never send them back into harm's way without protection.

Step 3: Provide Emotional Grounding

- Help survivor breathe slowly to reduce panic.
- Assure: *"You are safe right now. You are not alone."*
- If appropriate, read calming scripture (Psalm 91).

Step 4: Connect to Resources

- Shelters, hotlines, safe houses.
- Medical care for injuries or forensic exams.

- Legal aid for protective orders.

9.4 Crisis Intervention in Sexual Abuse Cases

If Abuse Was Recent

- Encourage immediate medical care for injuries and evidence collection.
- Reassure survivor they have the right to say "no" to invasive procedures if overwhelmed.
- Provide presence and prayer (if desired).

If Abuse is Ongoing

- Contact child protective services (if minor involved).
- Develop an exit plan with the survivor.
- Arrange ongoing trauma counseling.

Biblical Reflection:

The Good Samaritan (Luke 10:25–37) stopped to care for the wounded, providing immediate aid before long-term recovery. Crisis counseling is this first act of compassion.

9.5 Supporting Survivors in Legal Proceedings

Courtrooms and police stations can retraumatize survivors. Counselors can:

- Explain the process in advance.
- Offer to accompany them to hearings.
- Remind them: *"You are not the one on trial. You are the one seeking justice."*

Proverbs 31:8–9 reminds us: *"Speak up for those who cannot speak for themselves... defend the rights of the poor and needy."*

9.6 Pastoral Care in Crisis

For Christian counselors and pastors, spiritual support is essential during crises. Survivors often feel abandoned by God.

Practical Spiritual Support

- Pray short, simple prayers of safety.
- Share scriptures of refuge: *"God is our refuge and strength"* (Psalm 46:1).
- Avoid over-spiritualizing: do not tell them to "just forgive" in the middle of trauma.

9.7 Case Examples

Case 1: Immediate Escape

Elena (pseudonym), age 29, arrived at a counseling session with a black eye. She whispered that her partner had threatened to kill her if she left.

Counselor's Response:

- Assessed immediate danger.
- Called a domestic violence hotline and arranged safe shelter.
- Contacted police with Elena's consent.
- Prayed Psalm 23 over her as she left for safety.

Outcome: Elena found safety, and later began long-term counseling.

Case 2: Teen in Crisis

Marcus (pseudonym), age 16, disclosed suicidal thoughts due to ongoing abuse.

Counselor's Response:

- Stayed with Marcus until he was safe.
- Contacted emergency services.
- Notified child protective services (mandatory).
- Provided ongoing pastoral support once immediate risk was addressed.

Outcome: Marcus received inpatient care for stabilization, followed by ongoing therapy and discipleship support.

9.8 Reflection Questions for Counselors

1. Am I prepared to remain calm during a crisis situation?
2. Do I know the emergency hotlines and shelters in my area?
3. Am I confident in when and how to make a mandatory report?
4. How do I provide spiritual comfort without minimizing immediate danger?

9.9 Practical Tools for Chapter 9
Crisis Response Card (for Counselors)
Keep this handy in your Bible or notebook:

- Emergency Services: 911 (or local equivalent)
- Domestic Violence Hotline: 1-800-799-SAFE (U.S.)
- National Sexual Assault Hotline: 1-800-656-HOPE (U.S.)
- Local shelters: _____
- Legal aid contacts: _____

Emergency Grounding Prayer

"Lord Jesus, bring peace to this moment. Calm fear, protect from danger, and send Your angels of safety. Cover this child of Yours with Your refuge, in Jesus' name. Amen."

9.10 Closing Exhortation

Crisis moments are intense, unpredictable, and sacred. In those moments, the counselor becomes the hands and feet of Christ — offering protection, calm, and hope.

Isaiah 41:10 is a cornerstone promise for crisis care:

"Fear not, for I am with you; be not dismayed, for I am your God; I will strengthen you, I will help you, I will uphold you with my righteous right hand."

Counselors are not saviors, but they are called to be instruments of God's immediate help, guiding survivors from danger into safety, from despair into hope.

Chapter 10: Long-Term Healing and Restoration

Walking Survivors into Freedom, Identity, and Renewal

10.1 Introduction

After crisis has passed and safety is established, survivors begin the **long road of healing**. This process is not measured in days or weeks but often in **months and years**.

Healing requires:

- **Time** - allowing wounds to close at the survivor's pace.
- **Grace** - replacing shame with God's love.
- **Community** - safe relationships to rebuild trust.
- **Faith** - rediscovering God's goodness.

Jesus declared in **John 10:10**:
"The thief comes only to steal and kill and destroy; I came that they may have life and have it abundantly."

The counselor's role is to guide survivors beyond survival into **abundant living**.

10.2 The Journey of Forgiveness

Forgiveness Misunderstood

Survivors are often pressured into premature forgiveness. Counselors must carefully explain what forgiveness is and is not.

Forgiveness is:

- Releasing bitterness to God.
- Choosing freedom from resentment.
- A process, often gradual.

Forgiveness is NOT:

- Excusing abuse.
- Forgetting trauma.
- Reconciling with an unrepentant abuser.

Scripture: *"Be kind to one another, tenderhearted, forgiving one another, as God in Christ forgave you."* (Ephesians 4:32)

Practical Steps Toward Forgiveness

1. Acknowledge the full weight of the harm.
2. Grieve losses (Psalm 13).
3. Ask God for strength to forgive when ready.
4. Pray release: *"Lord, I give this person into Your hands."*

10.3 Renewing the Mind

Survivors often internalize lies: "I am worthless," "I am dirty," "God abandoned me." Long-term counseling must focus on **renewing the mind** with God's truth.

Romans 12:2: *"Do not be conformed to this world, but be transformed by the renewal of your mind."*

Practical Counseling Tools

- **Truth Journaling:** Write lies survivors believe, then replace them with scripture truths.
- **Scripture Meditation:** Daily reading of identity verses (e.g., Ephesians 1).
- **Affirmation Exercises:** Saying truths aloud: *"I am chosen. I am loved. I am clean."*

10.4 Rebuilding Trust in Relationships

Abuse shatters trust. Survivors must relearn how to build healthy, safe relationships.

Counselor's Guidance

- Encourage small steps - e.g., trusting one safe friend.
- Teach boundaries: saying "yes" and "no" with confidence.
- Normalize setbacks - trust takes time.
- Address relational patterns to prevent cycles of re-abuse.

Proverbs 3:5-6: *"Trust in the Lord with all your heart, and do not lean on your own understanding."*

10.5 Helping Survivors Reclaim Purpose

Abuse robs survivors of identity and calling. Long-term healing involves rediscovering **who God created them to be**.

Steps Toward Purpose

1. **Spiritual Renewal**: Reconnecting with God in prayer and worship.
2. **Gift Discovery**: Encouraging use of spiritual gifts (Romans 12:6-8).
3. **Service**: Helping others (support groups, ministry, advocacy).
4. **Life Goals**: Education, career, family dreams restored.

Jeremiah 29:11: *"For I know the plans I have for you… plans to give you a future and a hope."*

10.6 Case Examples

Case 1: Esther (Pseudonym)

Esther, a survivor of childhood sexual abuse, struggled for years with shame. Over time, counseling helped her replace lies with truth, memorize scripture, and forgive her abuser (without reconciliation).

Today, Esther mentors young women in her church, reclaiming her calling.

Case 2: David (Pseudonym)

David, who survived years of physical abuse, battled anger and mistrust. Counseling focused on grounding exercises, healthy boundaries, and prayer. Eventually, he began volunteering with at-risk youth, using his testimony as a tool for prevention.

10.7 Reflection Questions for Counselors

1. Do I pressure survivors to forgive too soon, or do I respect the process?
2. How am I helping survivors replace lies with biblical truth?
3. Do I encourage survivors to take steps toward community, or do I focus only on individual healing?
4. Am I helping survivors dream again about their future?
5.

10.8 Practical Tools for Chapter 10

Identity in Christ Worksheet

Survivors write "I am..." statements based on scripture:

- I am loved (John 3:16).
- I am chosen (1 Peter 2:9).
- I am free (John 8:36).
- I am clean (1 Corinthians 6:11).
- I am strong in Christ (Philippians 4:13).

Forgiveness Prayer Template

"Lord, I choose to release [Name]. I place them in Your hands. I release the bitterness, anger, and desire for revenge. Heal my heart and free me from this burden. In Jesus' name, Amen."

Long-Term Healing Plan

- Emotional healing goals (therapy, journaling).
- Spiritual healing goals (scripture study, prayer).
- Relational healing goals (building safe friendships).
- Life goals (career, ministry, education).

10.9 Closing Exhortation

Long-term healing is not linear. Survivors will face setbacks, flashbacks, and struggles. But with Christ at the center, healing is possible.

Philippians 1:6 promises:

"He who began a good work in you will carry it on to completion until the day of Christ Jesus."

The counselor's task is to walk alongside survivors in patience and faith, pointing them to the God who redeems all things and restores what was stolen.

Chapter 11: Special Populations

Adapting Counseling to Unique Needs

11.1 Introduction

While the principles of safety, validation, and healing remain the same, survivors' needs vary depending on age, gender, and cultural background. A skilled counselor recognizes that a "one-size-fits-all" approach is ineffective.

Paul said in **1 Corinthians 9:22**: *"I have become all things to all people, that by all means I might save some."* Likewise, counselors adapt their methods while remaining faithful to biblical truth.

11.2 Children and Adolescents

Unique Challenges

- Limited vocabulary to describe abuse.
- Fear of betraying family members.
- Dependence on adults for safety.
- May act out behaviorally instead of verbally.

Counseling Approaches

- Use simple, age-appropriate language ("safe touch," "unsafe touch").
- Encourage play therapy, art, or storytelling to express emotions.
- Reassure them repeatedly: *"It's not your fault."*
- Always involve protective services when abuse is disclosed.

Spiritual Care

- Teach that God loves children deeply (Matthew 19:14).

- Use stories like Joseph or Samuel to remind them that God calls young people for great purposes.

11.3 Male Survivors
Unique Challenges

- Stigma: "Men can't be victims."
- Pressure to appear strong.
- Difficulty expressing vulnerability.
- Struggles with sexual identity if abuse was same-sex.

Counseling Approaches

- Affirm masculinity is not diminished by being a victim.
- Address shame openly and directly.
- Encourage safe men's groups for support.
- Reframe strength through biblical manhood: *"Be strong and courageous"* (Joshua 1:9).

Spiritual Care

- Highlight stories of men who endured trauma (David, Job, Joseph).
- Reinforce that God values justice and healing for men as much as for women.

11.4 Elderly Survivors
Unique Challenges

- Often abused by caregivers or family members.

- May fear abandonment if they disclose.
- May depend on abuser for financial or physical care.
- Often underreported due to shame or isolation.

Counseling Approaches

- Listen patiently - many elders disclose slowly.
- Involve protective services for elder abuse.
- Encourage dignity and respect in care settings.

Spiritual Care

- Share scriptures of God's faithfulness in old age:
  - *"Even to your old age I am he, and to gray hairs I will carry you."* (Isaiah 46:4)
- Remind them they are still valuable and honored in God's kingdom.

11.5 Culturally Sensitive Counseling
Why Culture Matters

- Cultural norms shape how survivors understand abuse, family roles, and authority.
- Some cultures silence abuse to "protect family honor."
- Language barriers may make disclosure difficult.

Counseling Approaches

- Be aware of cultural stigma around abuse.
- Use interpreters or culturally appropriate support groups if needed.
- Avoid stereotypes or assumptions.

- Emphasize biblical truth over cultural distortions.

Acts 10:34 reminds us: *"God shows no partiality."* Healing is available to all cultures through Christ.

11.6 Case Examples

Case 1: A Child Survivor

Sophia, age 7, revealed abuse by an older cousin through drawings of "scary monsters." The counselor used art therapy to help her express feelings, reported the abuse, and reassured Sophia with Matthew 19:14. Over time, Sophia grew more secure in prayer and play.

Case 2: A Male Survivor

Carlos, age 35, disclosed abuse by a coach during his teens. He had never told anyone, fearing people would question his masculinity. The counselor affirmed him, helped him process his pain, and guided him to Psalm 27:1 ("The Lord is my light and my salvation; whom shall I fear?"). Carlos found strength in reclaiming his story.

Case 3: An Elder Survivor

Margaret, age 78, reported neglect and verbal abuse by her caregiver son. The counselor listened without judgment, reported to elder protective services, and reminded her of Isaiah 46:4. Margaret began to believe she still mattered to God.

11.7 Reflection Questions for Counselors

1. Do I unintentionally treat abuse as only a women's issue?
2. Am I trained to recognize non-verbal signs of abuse in children or elders?
3. How sensitive am I to cultural differences while still upholding biblical truth?
4. Do I make space for male survivors to share their stories without shame?

11.8 Practical Tools for Chapter 11
Child-Friendly Explanation of Abuse

- Good touch = helps, keeps you safe (hug from mom).
- Bad touch = hurts, makes you scared, secretive.
- Safe adults = people who listen and protect (teacher, counselor, police, pastor).

Affirmations for Men

- "Being abused does not make me weak."
- "God calls me His son and warrior."
- "I can be strong and still vulnerable."

Affirmations for Elders

- "I am still valuable."
- "God carries me even in old age."
- "My story matters."

11.9 Closing Exhortation

Abuse affects all ages, genders, and cultures, but God's healing is for all. Counselors must adapt approaches without compromising truth, meeting each survivor where they are.

Revelation 7:9 paints the picture of God's inclusive healing:

"A great multitude... from every nation, from all tribes and peoples and languages, standing before the throne and before the Lamb."

In God's kingdom, no survivor is forgotten. Each is precious, seen, and redeemed.

Chapter 12: The Counselor's Self-Care

Guarding Your Heart, Mind, and Spirit in Ministry

12.1 Introduction

Counseling survivors of abuse is rewarding, but it is also heavy work. Each story carries grief, pain, and injustice. Without intentional self-care, counselors can become emotionally drained, spiritually dry, or even retraumatized themselves.

Proverbs 4:23 reminds us:
"Above all else, guard your heart, for everything you do flows from it."

A burned-out counselor cannot guide survivors effectively. Self-care is not selfish, it is stewardship of the vessel God is using.

12.2 Recognizing Secondary Trauma

What is Secondary Trauma?

Secondary trauma (or vicarious trauma) occurs when counselors absorb the pain of survivors. Symptoms often mirror those of the survivor:

- Nightmares or intrusive thoughts.
- Emotional numbness or irritability.
- Feeling hopeless or spiritually distant.
- Difficulty separating work from personal life.

Signs of Burnout

- Constant fatigue.
- Cynicism or loss of empathy.
- Loss of joy in ministry.
- Withdrawing from prayer or fellowship.

Galatians 6:9 warns us:

"Let us not grow weary in doing good, for in due season we will reap, if we do not give up."

12.3 The Importance of Boundaries

Counselors must remember: *You are not the Savior - Christ is.* Your role is to guide, not to carry every burden.

Healthy Boundaries

- Limit availability (don't answer crisis calls at 2 a.m. unless prearranged).
- Keep professional distance - avoid over-identifying with a survivor's story.
- Do not counsel beyond your competence (refer to doctors, lawyers, therapists as needed).
- Maintain confidentiality but seek supervision when necessary.

Matthew 11:28–30 reminds us that *Jesus carries the heaviest yoke - not us.*

12.4 Spiritual Renewal for Counselors

Daily Practices

- Begin and end each day in prayer.
- Meditate on scripture, not just for sermons but for personal nourishment.
- Practice Sabbath rest (Exodus 20:8–10).
- Engage in worship outside of ministry responsibilities.

Prayer of Release (End of Day)

"Lord, I release every burden I carried today. I give back to You every story, every pain, every cry. You alone are the Healer. Refresh me with Your Spirit."

12.5 Emotional and Physical Self-Care

Emotional Practices

- Debrief with a mentor or supervisor after difficult sessions.
- Journal your own feelings (not just clients').
- Attend counseling yourself when needed.

Physical Practices

- Eat balanced meals, rest well, and exercise.
- Take breaks between heavy sessions.
- Use grounding techniques for yourself after hearing traumatic stories.

1 Corinthians 6:19–20 reminds us:
"Your body is a temple of the Holy Spirit... glorify God in your body."

12.6 Community and Support

Accountability

- Surround yourself with godly mentors.
- Join peer supervision groups for counselors.
- Stay connected to your church community.

Encouragement

Hebrews 10:24–25: *"Let us consider how to stir up one another to love and good works, not neglecting to meet together... but encouraging one another."*

12.7 Case Example

Case: Pastor John (Pseudonym)

John counseled multiple survivors weekly. Over time, he became weary, cynical, and short-tempered. He realized he was carrying burdens instead of releasing them to God.

Steps Taken:

- Began daily prayer of release.
- Took a three-month sabbatical for rest.
- Started meeting monthly with a mentor.
- Re-engaged in personal Bible study for refreshment.

Outcome: John returned renewed, able to counsel with fresh compassion.

12.8 Reflection Questions for Counselors

1. Do I recognize signs of secondary trauma in myself?
2. How do I release burdens to God instead of carrying them?
3. Am I practicing Sabbath rest, or am I constantly on call?
4. Do I have safe people to confide in when counseling becomes heavy?

12.9 Practical Tools for Chapter 12

Counselor's Self-Care Plan

- **Spiritual**: Daily prayer, scripture meditation, Sabbath rest.
- **Emotional**: Journaling, supervision, counseling when needed.
- **Physical**: Nutrition, exercise, sleep, breaks.
- **Relational**: Fellowship, mentorship, accountability partners.

Scriptures for Counselor Renewal

- *"Come to me, all who labor and are heavy laden, and I will give you rest."* (Matthew 11:28)
- *"The joy of the Lord is your strength."* (Nehemiah 8:10)
- *"He restores my soul."* (Psalm 23:3)

12.10 Closing Exhortation

Self-care is not optional - it is essential. A counselor who neglects themselves cannot pour into others. As Jesus often withdrew to pray (Luke 5:16), so must we.

Remember: **You are a vessel, not the source.** God is the source. Your task is to stay filled, renewed, and guarded so you can continue to bring His healing to others.

Chapter 13: Practical Tools and Resources

Equipping Counselors with Hands-On Materials

13.1 Introduction

Theories and strategies are important, but counselors also need **practical tools** they can immediately use in sessions. This chapter provides ready-to-use forms, worksheets, prayer guides, hotline numbers, and recommended resources for survivors and counselors alike.

Ecclesiastes 10:10 reminds us:

"If the ax is dull and one does not sharpen the edge, then he must use more strength; but wisdom brings success."

These tools are the sharpened edge of counseling ministry.

13.2 Sample Intake Form (Abuse Counseling)

Confidential Counseling Intake Form
Client Information

- Name: _____
- Age: _____ Gender: _____
- Contact Information: _____
- Emergency Contact: _____

Safety Questions

1. Do you feel safe at home? ☐ Yes ☐ No
2. Has anyone ever physically hurt you? ☐ Yes ☐ No
3. Has anyone ever touched you sexually without consent? ☐ Yes ☐ No

4. Do you fear anyone in your household or close circle? ☐ Yes ☐ No

Spiritual Questions

1. How would you describe your relationship with God right now?
2. Do you feel any spiritual struggles related to your experiences?
3. Would you like prayer included in your sessions? ☐ Yes ☐ No

13.3 Safety Planning Worksheet
My Safety Plan

1. **Safe People I Can Call:**
   -

-

1. **Safe Places I Can Go:**
   -

-

1. **Emergency Bag Contents:**
   - ID, keys, money, clothing, medications.
2. **Code Word for Danger:**
   -

1. **Important Phone Numbers:**

- Police/Emergency: _____
- Shelter Hotline: _____
- Trusted Friend/Relative: _____

Affirmation Scripture: *"God is our refuge and strength, an ever-present help in trouble."* (Psalm 46:1)

13.4 Survivor Journaling Prompts

- "One lie I believed because of abuse is _____. The truth from God's Word is _____."
- "Today I felt closest to God when _____."
- "One step of healing I took this week was _____."
- "A verse that gives me hope today is _____."

13.5 Affirmation and Identity in Christ Cards

Counselors can print these on small cards for survivors to carry:

- "I am fearfully and wonderfully made." (Psalm 139:14)
- "I am a new creation in Christ." (2 Corinthians 5:17)
- "I am washed, sanctified, and justified." (1 Corinthians 6:11)
- "I am chosen, holy, and dearly loved." (Colossians 3:12)
- "Nothing can separate me from God's love." (Romans 8:38–39)

13.6 Crisis and Hotline Resources

(U.S. Examples – Counselors should add their local numbers)

- **National Domestic Violence Hotline:** 1-800-799-SAFE (7233)

- **National Sexual Assault Hotline (RAINN):** 1-800-656-HOPE (4673)
- **Childhelp National Child Abuse Hotline:** 1-800-422-4453
- **National Suicide Prevention Lifeline:** 988
- **Elder Abuse Hotline:** 1-833-372-8311

(For international use: Counselors should gather local numbers for their country and add them to this section.)

13.7 Suggested Scriptures for Counseling

Comfort in Pain

- Psalm 34:18 – *"The Lord is near to the brokenhearted and saves the crushed in spirit."*
- Isaiah 41:10 – *"Fear not, for I am with you..."*

Healing and Renewal

- Isaiah 61:1–3 – *"He has sent me to bind up the brokenhearted..."*
- Joel 2:25 – *"I will restore to you the years that the locust has eaten."*

Identity in Christ

- Ephesians 1:4 – *"He chose us in him before the foundation of the world..."*
- Romans 8:1 – *"There is therefore now no condemnation for those who are in Christ Jesus."*

13.8 Reflection Questions for Counselors

1. Do I have safety plan templates and hotline numbers ready at all times?
2. Am I equipping survivors with tools they can take home (cards, prayers, worksheets)?
3. Am I continually learning through books and training, or relying only on past experience?
4. Do I have my own counselor/mentor for accountability and support?

13.9 Closing Exhortation

Counselors must not only bring wisdom and compassion but also **tangible resources** that survivors can hold, read, and use between sessions. These tools give survivors practical ways to continue healing beyond the counseling office.

Jesus gave both **words of comfort** and **actions of provision** (He fed the hungry, touched the sick, calmed storms). Likewise, counselors must combine **truth and tools** - words that heal and resources that protect.

Chapter 14: Conclusion and Commissioning

Equipped to Heal, Called to Stand

14.1 Introduction

This guide has walked through the journey of understanding abuse, counseling survivors, handling crisis, fostering long-term healing, and caring for yourself as a counselor. You now hold not only **knowledge** but also a **calling**.

The world is full of brokenness, but God has chosen you to be a vessel of healing. Survivors will come with shattered trust, heavy shame, and deep wounds. And you will meet them with the compassion of Christ, the wisdom of His Word, and the steadiness of His Spirit.

14.2 The Counselor's Mandate

1. **To See**
    - See what others ignore.
    - Recognize the hidden pain behind silence.
    - Notice the warning signs others dismiss.
2. **To Speak**
    - Speak truth to lies.
    - Break silence where secrecy reigns.
    - Defend the vulnerable who cannot defend themselves.
3. **To Shepherd**
    - Walk survivors gently through valleys of trauma.
    - Lead them beside still waters of God's peace (Psalm 23:2).
    - Restore their souls through patience and prayer.
4. **To Stand**

- Stand against evil and injustice.
- Stand in prayer when survivors cannot pray.
- Stand firm in faith, knowing God's power is greater than darkness.

14.3 Biblical Commissioning

Scripture commissions every counselor:

- *"He has sent me to bind up the brokenhearted, to proclaim freedom for the captives, and release from darkness for the prisoners."* (Isaiah 61:1)
- *"Defend the weak and the fatherless; uphold the cause of the poor and the oppressed."* (Psalm 82:3)
- *"Carry each other's burdens, and in this way you will fulfill the law of Christ."* (Galatians 6:2)

These verses remind us that this work is not optional but is central to the mission of Christ.

14.4 The Cost and the Reward

The Cost

- Emotional weight of hearing painful stories.
- Spiritual battles against oppression.
- Misunderstanding from those who minimize abuse.

The Reward

- Seeing lives restored.
- Witnessing God turn ashes into beauty (Isaiah 61:3).
- Hearing survivors testify: *"I once was bound, but now I am free."*

14.5 A Final Case Testimony

Case: Naomi (pseudonym)

Naomi, once silenced by years of sexual abuse, came into counseling broken, angry, and afraid. Through validation, prayer, trauma-focused care, and patient guidance, she slowly discovered her worth in Christ. Years later, Naomi became an advocate for other survivors, declaring: *"What Satan used to destroy me, God used to heal others."*

This is the vision: survivors becoming healers, victims becoming victors, silence turning into songs of freedom.

14.6 Reflection for the Counselor

- Am I willing to enter the hard places to bring hope?
- Do I trust God to carry the burdens I cannot?
- Am I ready to be both a listener and a warrior — gentle with the wounded, firm against injustice?

14.7 A Prayer of Commissioning

"Heavenly Father, I dedicate myself as Your servant in the ministry of healing. Use me to be a voice for the voiceless, a shelter for the vulnerable, and a guide for the wounded. Fill me with Your Spirit of wisdom, compassion, and courage. Guard my heart from weariness, my mind from fear, and my spirit from despair. May every survivor I counsel encounter Your love, Your truth, and Your freedom. In Jesus' name, Amen."

14.8 Final Exhortation

Counselors, you are stepping into holy ground. You will see pain few others see. But you will also witness the miracle of God's restoration. Never forget:

- You are not the healer - Jesus is.
- You are not the Savior - Christ alone saves.
- You are an instrument, a vessel, a channel of His hope.

Philippians 4:13 declares: *"I can do all things through Christ who strengthens me."*

That includes the hard, heartbreaking, but holy work of walking survivors into freedom.

Go forth equipped, empowered, and commissioned to bring light where darkness hides, to bring hope where despair dwells, and to bring healing where deep wounds remain.

Closing Remarks

Faithful to the Call of Healing and Protection

As you have walked through the pages of this guide, you have entered sacred ground—the reality of abuse, its devastating effects, and the holy calling of those who counsel and protect survivors. This is not light work. It is ministry at the heart of God's mission: to **bind up the brokenhearted, proclaim liberty to the captives, and comfort those who mourn** (Isaiah 61:1-3).

You, as a counselor, pastor, or caregiver, are invited to become:

- A **listening ear** where silence once prevailed.
- A **voice of truth** where lies have taken root.
- A **shield of safety** where fear has ruled.
- A **channel of hope** where despair has lingered.

Remember:

- Healing is a **journey, not an event**.
- Your role is not to "fix" the survivor, but to walk with them toward the One who heals completely - **Jesus Christ, the Great Physician**.
- You are not alone in this ministry. The Holy Spirit is your Counselor, Comforter, and Source of wisdom.

Galatians 6:9

"And let us not be weary in well doing: for in due season we shall reap, if we faint not."

When the road feels heavy, trust that your labor is not in vain. Every prayer, every word of encouragement, every moment spent listening is a seed of restoration planted in the life of someone deeply loved by God.

A Final Prayer

Heavenly Father,

Thank You for entrusting us with the sacred work of counseling and protecting the vulnerable. Give us courage when silence tempts us, wisdom when the path seems unclear, and compassion that reflects the heart of Christ. May every life touched by this ministry find healing, safety, and hope in You. Strengthen us to remain faithful until the day when every tear is wiped away, and Your perfect justice reigns forever. In Jesus' Name, Amen.

Homework Questions

Chapter 1 – Introduction to Counseling in Cases of Abuse

1. Why is it important for the church to address abuse openly?
2. According to Psalm 34:18, how does God respond to the brokenhearted?
3. In what ways does silence within the church contribute to cycles of abuse?
4. How can the counselor embody the compassion and justice of Christ?
5. What lessons can we learn from the story of Joseph as a victim of betrayal and injustice?

Chapter 2 – Understanding Physical and Sexual Abuse

1. What are some common misconceptions about abuse in Christian communities?
2. How would you define physical abuse? How would you define sexual abuse?
3. Why is it important to distinguish between biblical discipline and abuse?
4. How does Ephesians 5:11 guide us in addressing the reality of abuse?
5. What dangers exist when abuse is minimized or ignored in the church?

Chapter 3 – The Impact of Abuse on the Victim

1. How does abuse affect the emotional, physical, and spiritual dimensions of a person?
2. What kinds of lies do victims often believe about themselves after abuse?
3. How can Scripture be used to replace those lies with truth?
4. How do trauma responses (fear, shame, hypervigilance) manifest in daily life?
5. Why is patience crucial in helping a survivor heal?

Chapter 4 – The Profile of the Abuser

1. What are some common traits or tactics of abusers?
2. Why is manipulation such a powerful tool for abusers?
3. How do power and control play a role in abuse?
4. What biblical warnings address those who misuse authority?
5. How should the church respond when an abuser is identified?

Chapter 5 – Christian Counseling Principles for Survivors

1. Why is listening so important in counseling survivors of abuse?
2. How can counselors validate without judging?
3. Why is ensuring the safety of the victim always the top priority?
4. In what ways can Scripture be both helpful and harmful in

counseling?
5. How does the Good Samaritan serve as a model for abuse counseling?

Chapter 6 – Listening, Validating, and Creating Safe Spaces

1. What does it mean to truly listen with compassion?
2. Why is validation so healing for survivors?
3. What practical steps can create a physically and emotionally safe environment?
4. What mistakes should counselors avoid when listening to survivors?
5. How does the story of Jesus and the Samaritan woman (John 4) illustrate safe and restorative conversation?

Chapter 7 – Counseling Survivors of Sexual Abuse

1. Why does sexual abuse create such deep wounds in identity and dignity?
2. What lies do survivors of sexual abuse commonly believe, and how can we replace them with biblical truth?
3. What lessons can we learn from Tamar's story in 2 Samuel 13?
4. Why must counselors avoid pressuring survivors to share graphic details?
5. How can the church offer real support to survivors of sexual abuse?

Chapter 8 – Counseling Survivors of Physical Abuse

1. How is physical abuse different from healthy discipline?
2. What physical, emotional, and spiritual consequences come from physical abuse?
3. What lessons do we learn from David fleeing from Saul's violence?
4. Why must counselors encourage safety and not passive endurance in victims?
5. How can Scripture restore a victim's dignity after physical abuse?

Chapter 9 – Legal, Ethical, and Safety Issues

1. Why must counselors know and respect the laws regarding abuse?
2. What is the difference between confidentiality and "confidentiality with limits"?
3. How does Proverbs 31:8-9 instruct us to speak up for victims?
4. Why is it dangerous for a church to "handle abuse internally" without involving authorities?
5. How can counselors balance grace with justice in their role?

Chapter 10 – The Role of the Church and the Community of Faith

1. In what ways can the church become a refuge for survivors of

abuse?
2. How does the early church in Acts 6 serve as a model for caring for the vulnerable?
3. Why is enc covering abuse considered a sin before God?
4. What practical policies should every church have in place for protection?
5. How does Matthew 25:40 challenge us to view how we treat "the least of these"?

Chapter 11 – Family Counseling in Contexts of Abuse

1. How does abuse affect the entire family, not just the direct victim?
2. What generational cycles can abuse create if unaddressed?
3. How can truth-telling and open communication bring healing to families?
4. What lessons do we learn from Joseph's family restoration in Genesis 50?
5. What steps can help families rebuild trust and healthy roles?

Chapter 12 – Spiritual Healing and Restoration

1. How does abuse distort a survivor's view of God?
2. What steps can help a victim rebuild trust in the Lord?
3. How can Scripture be used to dismantle lies with truth?
4. What does Peter's restoration in John 21 teach us about new beginnings?
5. What role do prayer, worship, and community play in spiritual restoration?

Chapter 13 – Prevention, Education, and a Culture of Protection

1. Why is prevention better than reaction in cases of abuse?
2. What role does the family play in teaching boundaries and safety?
3. What should churches do to become truly safe spaces for children and vulnerable adults?
4. How does Nehemiah's rebuilding of Jerusalem's walls serve as a metaphor for protection?
5. What education strategies can empower children to speak up against abuse?

Chapter 14 – The Pah to Complete Restoration

1. What does "complete restoration" mean in Christ?
2. Why is healing a gradual process and not an instant event?
3. How can survivors move from victimhood to living with purpose?
4. What lessons does Job's story teach us about God's ability to restore?
5. How can pain be transformed into ministry?

Epilogue
A Final Call to the Christian Counselor

Counseling victims of physical and sexual abuse is not merely a ministry assignment, it is sacred ground. Those who have endured abuse carry wounds that are often invisible yet profoundly deep. To walk with them is to step into a space that requires humility, courage, wisdom, and an unwavering dependence on the Holy Spirit.

This guide was written with one central conviction: God sees, God cares, and God restores. Every survivor matters to Him, and He entrusts counselors, pastors, and leaders with the holy responsibility of reflecting His compassion and justice.

Isaiah 61:1 (NKJV)

"The Lord has anointed Me to heal the brokenhearted, to proclaim liberty to the captives."

May this book serve as a reminder that your presence, your listening, and your faithfulness can become instruments of healing in the hands of God.

Pastoral Conclusion

Abuse thrives in secrecy, silence, and fear but it loses its power when exposed to truth, light, and justice. The Church of Jesus Christ must never be a place of concealment, denial, or protection of wrongdoing. It must be a refuge for the wounded and a defender of the vulnerable.

This manual calls counselors and leaders to:

- Protect victims, not institutions
- Believe survivors, not silence them
- Uphold justice without abandoning grace
- Reflect Christ without compromise

Proverbs 31:8–9

"Speak up for those who cannot speak for themselves… defend the rights of the poor and needy."

Faithful counseling is not passive—it is courageous, compassionate, and obedient to the heart of God.

Final Prayer for Counselors

Lord Jesus,

You are the Shepherd of the wounded and the Defender of the oppressed.

Grant me wisdom beyond my own understanding, courage to speak truth, and compassion that reflects Your heart.

Guard me from fear, complacency, and silence.

Use me as an instrument of healing, protection, and restoration.

May every life I serve encounter Your hope and redemption.

In Your holy name, Amen.

Final Reflections

Every restored life is a testimony of God's redemptive power. As a counselor, your obedience and faithfulness may be the turning point between lifelong suffering and renewed hope.

Matthew 25:40

"Whatever you did for one of the least of these brothers and sisters of mine, you did for Me."

May this guide remain a living tool in your hands, and may Christ remain your greatest Counselor.

ABOUT THE AUTHOR
Dr. Greg Wood

Dr. Greg Wood is a missionary, educator, pastor, and Christian counselor with decades of ministry experience dedicated to leadership development, biblical education, and the protection and restoration of vulnerable lives.

He is the Director of Fountain of Life Theological Institute International, where he has trained pastors, counselors, and ministry leaders across cultures and nations. As a second-generation missionary, Dr. Wood has devoted much of his life to serving in Latin America, with a special focus on theological education, discipleship, and healing ministry.

Dr. Wood is also deeply involved in humanitarian and restorative work, including advocacy for abused, neglected, and vulnerable individuals. His ministry reflects a commitment to biblical truth, pastoral integrity, and practical compassion.

Through his teaching, writing, and leadership, Dr. Wood seeks to equip the Church to respond faithfully to the brokenhearted - combining sound theology, ethical responsibility, and Christ-centered care.

Author's Mission Statement

"My calling is to equip leaders and counselors who will protect the vulnerable, proclaim truth without fear, and walk with the broken toward healing and restoration in Christ."

Don't miss out!

Visit the website below and you can sign up to receive emails whenever Dr. Greg Wood publishes a new book. There's no charge and no obligation.

https://books2read.com/r/B-A-GGWME-ONNXI

BOOKS 2 READ

Connecting independent readers to independent writers.

www.ingramcontent.com/pod-product-compliance
Lightning Source LLC
Chambersburg PA
CBHW050653160426
43194CB00010B/1923